A Fox and His Box

by Marj Milano
illustrated by Deborah Colvin Borgo

Practice Decodable 29

McGraw Hill Education

Bothell, WA • Chicago, IL • Columbus, OH • New York, NY

MHEonline.com

Send all inquiries to:
McGraw-Hill Education
8787 Orion Place
Columbus, OH 43240

ISBN: 978-0-02-145325-2
MHID: 0-02-145325-X

Printed in China

8 9 10 11 12 DSS 27 26 25 24 23

“The box is a trap,” said Fox.

"It can trap a dog," said Fox.

"It can trap a cat," said Fox.

"It can't trap a big ox," said Fox.

"It can't trap fast rabbits!" said Rabbit.

"The box can't trap rabbits," said Fox.